Oprah Winfrey

Jennifer Strand

abdopublishing.com

Published by Abdo Zoom™, PO Box 398166, Minneapolis, Minnesota 55439. Copyright © 2017 by Abdo Consulting Group, Inc. International copyrights reserved in all countries. No part of this book may be reproduced in any form without written permission from the publisher. Abdo Zoom™ is a trademark and logo of Abdo Consulting Group, Inc.

Printed in the United States of America, North Mankato, Minnesota
072016
092016

 THIS BOOK CONTAINS
RECYCLED MATERIALS

Cover Photo: Chris Pizzello/AP Images
Interior Photos: Chris Pizzello/AP Images, 1; Brian Zak/Sipa Press/metgala_bz.104/1005041206, 4; Jeremy Piper/AP Images, 5, 12–13; Seth Poppel/Yearbook Library, 6, 7; Charlie Knoblock/AP Images, 8–9; Charles Bennett/AP Images, 10; Charles Bennet/AP Images, 11; Chris Weeks/AP Images, 14; Evan Agostini/ImageDirect/Getty Images, 15; Ben Rose/WireImage/Getty Images, 16–17, 18–19; Mark J. Terrill/AP Images, 18

Editor: Brienna Rossiter
Series Designer: Madeline Berger
Art Direction: Dorothy Toth

Publisher's Cataloging-in-Publication Data
Names: Strand, Jennifer, author.
Title: Oprah Winfrey / by Jennifer Strand.
Description: Minneapolis, MN : Abdo Zoom, [2017] | Series: Great women |
    Includes bibliographical references and index.
Identifiers: LCCN 2016941352 | ISBN 9781680792249 (lib. bdg.) |
    ISBN 9781680793925 (ebook) | 9781680794816 (Read-to-me ebook)
Subjects: LCSH: Winfrey, Oprah--Juvenile literature. | Television personalities--
    Biography--Juvenile literature. | African American television personalities--
    Biography--Juvenile literature. | Actors--United States--Biography--Juvenile
    literature. | African American actors--Biography--Juvenile literature.
Classification: DDC 791.4502/8092 [B]--dc23
LC record available at http://lccn.loc.gov/2016941352

Table of Contents

Introduction

Oprah Winfrey is a
TV star and **producer**.

She hosted *The Oprah Winfrey Show* for many years. It was the most successful **talk show** ever.

Early Life

Oprah was born on January 29, 1954. Her family was poor. She moved a lot.

She was often unhappy.
But she did well in school.
She liked public speaking.

Rise to Fame

Winfrey became a radio news **reporter**. In 1978 she co-hosted a TV show.

It was called
People Are Talking.

Winfrey **interviewed** people. She was warm and friendly. This made her easy to talk to.

The show quickly
became a success.

Superstar

In 1984 Winfrey became the host of a talk show.

It was renamed *The Oprah Winfrey Show* in 1985. People all over the world watched it.

Winfrey was a producer for other TV shows and movies. She was also an actress.

She started a
magazine, too.

Legacy

Winfrey featured people who solved problems. She encouraged people to read books.

Many people watched her shows. They trusted her opinions.

The Oprah Winfrey Show ended in 2011. But Winfrey is still famous.

She owns many businesses. She also gives much of her money away.

Oprah Winfrey

Born: January 29, 1954

Birthplace: Kosciusko, Mississippi

Known For: Winfrey was the host of *The Oprah Winfrey Show.* She owns many businesses, including a TV network and a magazine.

Key 📅 Dates

1954: Oprah Gail Winfrey is born on January 29.

1978: Winfrey starts co-hosting *People Are Talking*.

1985-2011: Winfrey hosts *The Oprah Winfrey Show*.

2000: Winfrey starts a magazine.

2008: The Oprah Winfrey Network is formed.

2013: Winfrey receives the Presidential Medal of Freedom.

Glossary

interviewed - asked someone questions.

producer - a person who is in charge of making a movie, TV show, or music album.

reporter - a person who searches for information and then presents it to the public.

talk show - a TV show in which a host talks with guests or audience members.

Booklinks

For more information
on **Oprah Winfrey**, please visit
booklinks.abdopublishing.com

Z**m In on Biographies!**

Learn even more with the Abdo Zoom
Biographies database. Check out
abdozoom.com for more information.

Index